All About
Indonesia

Stories, Songs and Crafts for Kids

Written and Illustrated by
Linda Hibbs

TUTTLE Publishing

Tokyo | Rutland, Vermont | Singapore

Published by Tuttle Publishing, an imprint of
Periplus Editions (HK) Ltd.

www.tuttlepublishing.com

Library of Congress Cataloging-in-Publication data for
this title is in progress.

ISBN 978-0-8048-4085-9

Distributed by

North America, Latin America & Europe
Tuttle Publishing
364 Innovation Drive, North Clarendon,
VT 05759-9436 U.S.A.
Tel: 1 (802) 773-8930; Fax: 1 (802) 773-6993
info@tuttlepublishing.com; www.tuttlepublishing.com

Japan
Tuttle Publishing
Yaekari Building, 3rd Floor 5-4-12 Osaki,
Shinagawa-ku Tokyo 141 0032
Tel: (81) 3 5437-0171; Fax: (81) 3 5437-0755
sales@tuttle.co.jp; www.tuttle.co.jp

Asia Pacific
Berkeley Books Pte. Ltd.
61 Tai Seng Avenue #02-12, Singapore 534167
Tel: (65) 6280-1330; Fax: (65) 6280-6290
inquiries@periplus.com.sg; www.periplus.com

Indonesia
PT Java Books Indonesia
Kawasan Industri Pulogadung
Jl Rawa Gelam IV No.9, Jakarta 13930
Tel: (62) 21 4682-1088; Fax: (62) 21 461-0206
crm@periplus.co.id; www.periplus.com

First edition
16 15 14 13   10 9 8 7 6 5 4 3 2 1   1310EP
Printed in Hong Kong

TUTTLE PUBLISHING® is a registered trademark of
Tuttle Publishing, a division of Periplus Editions (HK) Ltd

The Tuttle Story
"Books to Span the East and West"

Many people are surprised when they learn that the world's
largest publisher of books on Asia had its beginnings in the
tiny American state of Vermont. The company's founder,
Charles Tuttle, came from a New England family steeped in
publishing, and his first love was books—especially old and
rare editions.

Tuttle's father was a noted antiquarian dealer in Rutland,
Vermont. Young Charles honed his knowledge of the trade
working in the family bookstore, and later in the rare books
section of Columbia University Library. His passion for
beautiful books—old and new—never wavered through his
long career as a bookseller and publisher.

After graduating from Harvard, Tuttle enlisted in the
military and in 1945 was sent to Tokyo to work on General
Douglas MacArthur's staff. He was tasked with helping to
revive the Japanese publishing industry, which had been
utterly devastated by the war. After his tour of duty was
completed, he left the military, married a talented and
beautiful singer, Reiko Chiba, and in 1948 began several
successful business ventures.

To his astonishment, Tuttle discovered that postwar Tokyo
was actually a book-lover's paradise. He befriended dealers
in the Kanda district and began supplying rare Japanese
editions to American libraries. He also imported American
books to sell to the thousands of GIs stationed in Japan. By
1949, Tuttle's business was thriving, and he opened Tokyo's
very first English-language bookstore in the Takashimaya
Department Store in Ginza, to great success. Two years later,
he began publishing books to fulfill the growing interest of
foreigners in all things Asian.

Though a westerner, Charles Tuttle was hugely
instrumental in bringing knowledge of Japan and Asia to a
world hungry for information about the East. By the time of
his death in 1993, he had published over 6,000 books on
Asian culture, history and art—a legacy honored by Emperor
Hirohito in 1983 with the "Order of the Sacred Treasure," the
highest honor Japan bestows upon non-Japanese.

The Tuttle company today maintains an active backlist of
some 1,500 titles, many of which have been continuously
in print since the 1950s and 1960s—a great testament to
Charles Tuttle's skill as a publisher. More than 60 years after
its founding, Tuttle Publishing is as active today as at any
time in its history, still inspired by Charles' core mission—to
publish fine books to span the East and West and provide a
greater understanding of each.

CONTENTS

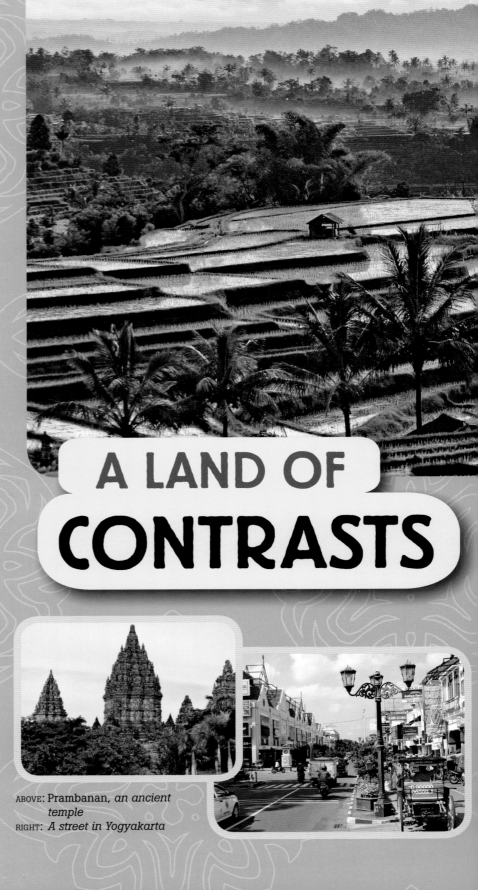

A majestic volcano rising above the clouds

A LAND OF
CONTRASTS

Arriving in Indonesia via plane and looking down on some of its 17,000 islands with volcanoes rising majestically above the white clouds, is like arriving in a magical place with giants' stepping stones.

Indonesia is a land of contrasts. One minute you can be walking past ancient temples built thousands of years ago and the next minute you find yourself looking up at brand new modern buildings reaching for the sky. You can see people in traditional costume next to those wearing jeans and a t-shirt. If you want a snack, you can drop into a supermarket similar to ones in your own town—or buy from someone pushing a little cart down the street. There is never a dull moment when you walk along the busy footpaths with hundreds of others, or dash across the busy road avoiding motorbikes, cars and horse and

ABOVE: Prambanan, *an ancient temple*
RIGHT: *A street in Yogyakarta*

TOP: *A modern supermarket*
ABOVE: *A street vendor*

Life in Indonesia is influenced by the hot and humid weather. There is no winter, spring or summer. There are wet and dry seasons but it is hot and humid all year long. During the wet season, dark clouds gather in the afternoon and bring torrential downpours of rain. Rainwater gushes down the streets, people scramble for shelter or hurriedly throw waterproof sheets over themselves as they ride by on their motorbikes. The rain often departs as suddenly as it arrives. The sun shines through the clouds and glistens on the water drenched streets and within moments the scene is as busy as it was before.

carts. Step outside town and the scene is transformed into lush green rice fields and swaying coconut palms. Just when you think you are in the most peaceful place on earth—a large and noisy bus roars past on its journey elsewhere.

SAY IT
IN BAHASA INDONESIA...

Hallo	Hello
Selamat pagi	Good morning
Terima kasih	Thank you

DID YOU KNOW?

Population of Indonesia: **240 million**
Captial city: **Jakarta**

Comparisons:

Population of Australia: **about 23 million**
Population of China: **about 1.35 billion**
Population United Kingdom: **about 63 million**
Population of the USA: **about 317 million**

Do you know how many islands are in Indonesia?

About 17,000.

Wow! Do people live on all of them?

No, some of the islands are too small. Only we *cicaks* can live on them!

Jakarta, the capital of Indonesia

THE CITY OF JAKARTA

Busy street in Jakarta

Jakarta is the capital city of Indonesia and is found on the island of Java. The streets are bustling with life. The thousands of cars create big traffic jams each morning as people try to get to work. Small street stalls on the pavements are dwarfed below the tall skyscrapers. Buses jostle with cars as a tiny *bajaj* zips past. These noisy three-wheeled motor vehicles, with just enough room for a driver in front and two passengers squeezing into the small space

DID YOU KNOW?

When the Dutch ruled Indonesia, they renamed Jakarta, Batavia.

behind, are rarely found outside Jakarta. Look beyond the busy streets and you will find fascinating museums and harbors with majestic sailing boats. Jakarta is the travel gateway to other islands—and to the world. There are ferries in the harbor, bus terminals and large train stations and a busy international airport. Jakarta is the center of government and business, a starting place for many travelers, and a home to many people both rich and poor.

The Monas monument houses a museum underneath.

Going shopping

In the big cities of Indonesia you can wander through large expensive shopping malls or seek out smaller shops that specialize in latest fashions, toys, or food to cook for dinner. Some of the small shops or businesses that line the streets offer a wide range of services such as fixing motorbikes, making furniture or selling electrical goods. You can also buy things such as magazines, bags or pens from the many stalls that can be found along the street pavements.

Markets are where everyone buys their fruit, vegetables and meat. Markets also offer a treasure trove of interesting things from fancy hair clips to CDs.

Markets offer a little bit of everything.

A typical Indonesian village

VILLAGE LIFE

TOP: *Primary school children walking to school in a village*

ABOVE: *Rice fields surround the villages*

Village life is more relaxed than city life. Villages are usually set amongst the rice fields with coconut palms and other productive plants surrounding the houses. The Lurah (head of the village) makes sure that the village's activities and production run smoothly.

Villagers work hard to maintain their crops and sell their produce. Juicy mangoes, fragrant paw paws and sweet pineapples are just a few of the tropical fruits that can be eaten fresh, made into delicious drinks or sold at the local market.

SAY IT
IN BAHASA INDONESIA...

Kota	City
Desa	Village
Saya tinggal di kota.	I live in the city.

Rice planting and harvesting

Indonesia's main crop is rice. The green rice fields can be seen almost everywhere. Sometimes these are flat fields and at other times they are tiered on levels up the side of a hill. Steamed rice is eaten with most meals each day. The meals are hot and spicy.

Rice growing starts with plowing the fields, usually with a buffalo or two pulling the plow. When the fields fill with water from the heavy wet season rains the seedlings are ready to plant in rows. When the plants are fully grown they are cut and the seed (rice grains) are shaken or beaten from the stalks.

DID YOU KNOW?

Cassava is a common food grown in villages. Tapioca is made from cassava root starch. You might have tried pearl tapioca, made into a pudding, sweetened with sugar and served with milk. In Indonesia they eat lots of cassava, but only sometimes sweetened with palm sugar and coconut milk. *Singkong* (cassava) is more often cooked and served like potato, or ground into a flour and made into "chips." The leaves are boiled or steamed and served as a side dish.

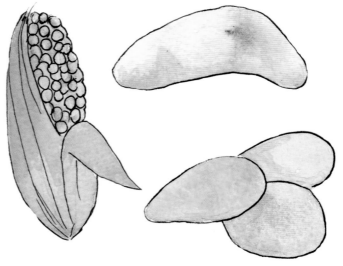

Food from typical crops grown in a village: Sweet corn, sweet potato and mango

A surfer glides over waves in Kuta, Bali.

THE SEA

Surfers go to Bali and Sumatra to catch the waves. In the smooth waters around many of the islands, small sailing boats called Perahu—used for fishing or short-distance travel—can be seen with their colorful sails catching the wind. Scuba divers floating through the warm tropical waters see beautiful coral reefs and all kinds of colorful

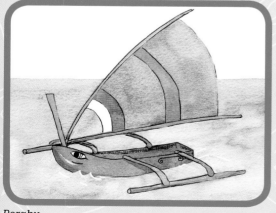

Perahu

Come closer so we can greet each other properly

Hati-hati! Ada udang di balik batu!

*"**Hati-hati! Ada udang di balik batu!**" is an Indonesian proverb that means "Be careful! There's a prawn on the other side of the stone!" It's used to express that there are hidden motives behind someone's actions. What other motive did the komodo have?*

DID YOU KNOW?

The Komodo dragon is the largest lizard in the world and lives on the island of Komodo in eastern Indonesia. The Komodo eats small animals and fish. They can also swim and in the past were known to swim between smaller islands looking for food.

TOP: *White sand beach in Bali*
ABOVE: *Black sand beach in Java*

fish. The turtle (including the Green and Leatherback turtles) also swims in these waters.

The sea is a source of food for the local people and famous as a trade route between islands. It also sometimes has a dangerous side, as was seen from the devastation when a tsunami hit the coast of Sumatra in 2010.

Being surrounded by sea, there are lots of beaches in Indonesia. Some consist of black sand—a combination of normal sand and minerals from ancient volcanic eruptions. Other beaches have beautiful white sand and palm trees.

But I thought my mountain was the only one!

THE MOUNTAINS

The giant steppingstones—volcanoes that rise out of many of the islands of Indonesia—are part of what is known as the "Pacific Ring of Fire." Despite the danger, the local people are used to living with volcanoes. Many villages are quite close to the mountain because the soil is rich for growing crops. Lush tropical forests cover the slopes and the air is fresh and cool.

There are over 400 volcanoes in Indonesia. Around 100 of these are still active.

Gunung Merapi

Krakatau

On August 27, 1883 the world shook when the volcano Krakatau that lies between the islands of Java and Sumatra erupted. Large rocks were thrown into the air and hit the decks of sailing ships as well as the land and sea. Nearly 40,000 people were killed. Volcanic ash soared more than 22 miles into the sky and circled around the world for several years, causing amazingly vivid sunsets from the dust particles in the air.

DID YOU KNOW?

The sound of the Krakatau explosion was heard in northern Australia and barometers went crazy in Washington D.C and around the world.

Krakatau erupting in May 2008

Gunung Merapi (Mt. Merapi) is an active volcano only 25 km from the town of Yogyakarta in Central Java. Sometimes at night you can see the very tip of the mountain glowing red as lava slips down its slopes. At other times the volcano produces deadly steam clouds that burn everything in its path.

A closeup of Gunung Merapi's steaming peaks

Make your own volcano

You can make your own miniature volcanic eruption. Make sure you do this outside!

- Create a volcano mountain shape out of plaster of paris or clay.
- Insert a small specimen jar or other narrow container in the top and leave the hole open.
- Wait till the plaster of paris or clay dries then paint it green, blue and brown.
- Pour two teaspoons of baking soda and a couple drops of red food coloring into the container Pour ¼ cup of vinegar into the container.
- Stand back and watch your volcano erupt!

AND THE FORESTS

Lush tropical forests are found at the base of most Indonesian mountains and along the many rivers that flow through each island. In the forests, large jungle trees with vines grow alongside beautiful flowers such as the hibiscus and fragrant frangipani. There is also a rich array of wildlife such as the magnificent bird of paradise, the orangutan and the elephant. While tigers no longer live in the

SAY IT
IN BAHASA INDONESIA...

pantai	beach
hutan	forest
harimau	tiger
orangutan	orang utang
badak	rhinoceros
burung	bird
monyet	monkey

forests of Java and Bali, they can still be found in forests on Sumatra and Kalimantan. There is also a small mouse deer called kancil.

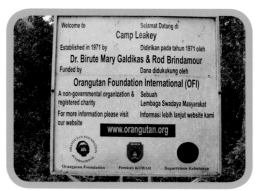

Protecting the Orangutan

Many of the forests where the orangutans live have been destroyed to make way for crops or buildings. In order to maintain what is left of their natural habitat, special parks have been set up where they can live without being threatened. The orangutan is now a protected species worldwide. Several rehabilitation centers have been set up in Sumatra and Kalimantan, like Camp Leakey, where injured orangutans are cared for before returning to the wild.

Save the Orangutan (UK): www.savetheorangutan.co.uk
Australian Orangutan Project: www.orangutan.org.au
Borneo Orangutan survival: www.orangutans.com.au
Orang utan foundation: www.orangutanfoundation.
wildlifedirect.org
World Wildlife Fund: www.worldwildlife.org

DID YOU KNOW?

The word "orangutan" means "person of the forest" and comes from two Indonesian words: *orang*, meaning "person" and *hutan* meaning "forest."

I don't want to live in a zoo! I'd rather live in the forest!

Many stories are told in Indonesia and Malaysia about the timid and yet cunning kancil (pronounced "kan-chil") or mouse deer.

Not related to mice, and only distantly related to deer, they have hooves and are about the size of a rabbit. A kancil's legs are as thin as a pencil.

THE STORY OF KANCIL

One day Kancil was trotting quietly through the forest. She was feeling very hungry and so far had had no luck finding food on her side of the river. She looked longingly over to the other side of the river and glimpsed rich fruit that made her mouth water.

She trotted down to the river's edge and was just about to hop on a log to carry her over when suddenly the log moved! Buaya, the crocodile rose to the surface and grabbed her leg in a flash. Squealing with fright Kancil tried to free herself. She was known for her cunning but she would have to think fast to get out of this alive and maybe still have a chance to eat that delicious fruit on the other side.

Suddenly Kancil found her voice. "Buaya you are such a big and strong animal. I cannot possibly satisfy your appetite," she said. "If I bring my family to you – my strong husband and children—then you have the chance to catch four instead of one kancil. The trouble is," she continued, "They swam across to the other side this morning. I was just going to meet them so we could return home together."

Buaya felt annoyed and slashed his tail in frustration. His friends had warned him about Kancil's cleverness but this all sounded fine. If Kancil made and kept the promise then he'd have a nice belly full of food.

"I'll take you across the river if you promise to return with your family."

"Of course I promise," Kancil quickly replied. "Our house is on this side, so how could we not return?"

Kancil stepped carefully onto the crocodile's back and traveled across to the other side of the river. She leapt lightly and landed on the riverbank. Kancil could already smell the beautiful aroma of the fruit that awaited her.

From the safety of the trees she turned around, and with laughter in her voice she said,

"You silly Buaya. My family didn't swim over the river this morning! But thanks for taking me across the river...now I can eat as much fruit as I like."

The Buaya felt his own tummy groan with hunger and thrashed his tail about in anger. In the distance he saw Kancil prancing and jumping through the forest and knew that he had been tricked. And Kancil knew that when it was time to return...she could easily trick another crocodile!

DID YOU KNOW?

The story of kancil is used in shadow puppet performances in Indonesia. Go to page 54 and you will find more information and how to make your own kancil and buaya puppet.

My name is Vita. I am 10 years old and I go to Primary school. I start getting ready for school at 6:15 in the morning.

GOING TO SCHOOL

G oing to school in Indonesia means getting up very early in the morning. Some schools start at 7:30. The students attend school during the coolest part of the day. Most schools end the day around lunchtime. In areas where there is a shortage of schools some children go to school in the morning and some in the afternoon.

Primary schools in Indonesia are called *Sekolah Dasar*. They range from Grades 1–6. Secondary school is divided into Junior High and Senior High school.

In Indonesia primary school children wear a red and white uniform. On Saturdays students might dress in their sports uniform. Indonesian schools are similar to schools all over the world. An Indonesian classroom may have more students than yours, and students sit at traditional double wooden desks with lids rather than at tables or individual desks. The children might not have quite the same technology or sports equipment your school has but they learn many of the same kind of things.

My school building

y brother Jono rides his bike to chool. He goes to high school.

My friends are playing a game before lining up for class.

Some of my friends play soccer at school.

Each island has its own language in Indonesia, and each region of an island does too. For example, not only do the people of Sumatra and Java speak different languages but the people in West Java speak a different language from those in the East. Imagine how hard it must have been for Indonesians to understand each other.

Hai. Apa kabar? Nama saya Iwan. Saya suka bermain bola basket.

THE INDONESIAN LANGUAGE

Apa kabar?

Baik.

DID YOU KNOW?

Shaking hands with your right hand when you greet someone in Indonesia is very important for both men and women. To not shake hands can be insulting. Rather than a handshake, the traditional Indonesian Islamic greeting involves gently taking the other person's hands in your hands then waving your right hand towards your heart (towards left shoulder).

Bahasa Indonesia

Everyone still speaks their regional language, but they also speak the national language, called Bahasa Indonesia, which was introduced in the 1950s to help everyone communicate with each other across the islands. It is based partly on the Malay language, but also incorporates local languages as well as some words from Dutch, Arabic and English.

Bahasa Indonesia

Indonesian words are spelled the way they sound—so much easier than English! The vowel sounds (**a**, **e**, **i**, **o**, **u**) are softer than in English.

Here are some hints that can help you speak Indonesian well
Depending on the length of the word, syllables (groups of letters) in Indonesian words are either pronounced equally or some given more emphasis than others.
For example:

Nama (two syllables **na**-ma)   more emphasis is given to the first syllable **na**.
Selamat (three syllables se-**la**-mat)   more emphasis is given to the middle syllable.
If there are more syllables   emphasis is given to the second last syllable.

Here are some simple questions and answers:

Siapa namamu?   What is your name?
Nama saya Aden   My name (is) Aden :)

Try learning these words and sentences:

Keluarga   family
Nama Ibu saya Helen.   My mom's name is Helen.
Nama Bapak saya Peter.   My dad's name is Peter.
Nama teman saya Katie.   My friend's name is Katie.
Saya suka bermain bola basket.   I like basket ball.
Saya tidak suka tenis.   I don't like tennis.

Now that you know how to put some words together in a sentence—try using some of the words presented on the pages "Say it in Indonesian."'

Getting up very early each morning is important for many people in Indonesia. It is not only essential for those who follow the Islamic religion (see p. 31) but also a way of avoiding the main heat of the day. By sunrise a farmer has already checked his animals and taken the fruit and vegetables to market to sell. By 7.00 AM the market is bustling and shops and schools are opening. By early afternoon, as the heat intensifies, schools often finish and even some workers take a short sleep known as *tidur siang*.

When Vita comes home from school sometimes she sleeps or plays with her little brother or helps her mom around

Vita helps her mom cook dinner.

EVERYDAY LIFE

You're not meant to get into the tub!

the house. Sometimes, when it is very hot, everyone in the house sleeps for a while.

Vita takes a wash—or has a *mandi*, as it is known in Indonesia—twice a day. A *mandi* consists of a large built-in tub of water in a bathroom with a well drained floor. You pour the cold water over you with a plastic dipper. The feel of the water in the cool of the morning makes Vita shiver but in the hot afternoon the water comes as a refreshing relief. After her *mandi* she brushes her teeth.

Waterbom in Bali is popular with local and overseas tourists. Children love slipping down the many different slippery slides and splashing into the water.

ON THE
WEEKENDS....

ABOVE: *Locals never tire of the islands' beautiful beaches.*

RIGHT: *Many children and teenagers in Indonesia like to play guitar and sing. They also like going to hear their favorite bands perform.*

In their spare time Indonesian children play games or go places with their family just like you probably do. Some children love to skateboard, some play computer games, while others prefer more traditional games. Sports such as tennis, basketball or soccer are also popular. On weekends families might visit friends, take a trip to a mountain or beach or have fun at places like the entertainment park, Jaya Ancol in Jakarta or Water Bom in Bali.

Gelora Bung Karno Stadium during soccer match between Indonesia vs South Korea in 2007 AFC Asian Cup in Jakarta

SAY IT
IN BAHASA INDONESIA...

hobi	hobby
bermain	to play
sepak bola	soccer
tenis	tennis
bermain papan roda	skateboarding
berlayang-layang	to fly kites
akhir minggu	weekend

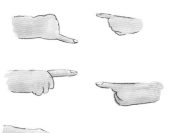

Traditional Games

Handclapping games, knuckles, games using pebbles on a special board (*dakon*) as well as a variation of the rock, paper, scissors game, known as *semut, gajah, orang* (ant, elephant, person) can all be found in Indonesia. *Takraw* is a game boys play with ball made of woven rattan (type of dried grass). Players use their feet to kick the ball over a net. No hands can be used. *Pencak Silat* is a popular martial art, especially in West Java. In the dry season kite makers are very busy making beautifully designed kites that children love to fly.

A girl playing jacks

A boy playing Dakon

A GLIMPSE
INTO THE PAST

Prambanan, an ancient Hindu temple in Java

Ancient temples

Indonesia was once ruled by ancient Kingdoms. Ruins from the time of these kingdoms can still be found in some parts of the country.

Borobudur

The ancient Buddhist temple, Borobudur, is a magnificent monument built from stones in the 8th Century. There are several flights of stone stairs—wall carvings that tell stories and hundreds of statues of Buddha lining the top part of the structure. Borobudur was apparently

DID YOU KNOW?

On Borobudur monument, the stupas (statue of Buddha sitting in lotus position) can be found under bell-like structures. As you climb the main steps of the monument, if you reach in and touch the first stupa you come across, it is said to bring you good luck.

Borobudur

abandoned not long after completion and became covered in ash and dirt from near-by volcano, Mt. Merapi. The volcanic ash was only cleared in 1815 to reveal the true size and magnitude of Borubudur.

Prambanan
Prambanan temple is an ancient group of Hindu temples built some time between the 8th and 10th Centuries. These temples were built from stone and also contain carvings of stories that relate to ancient Hindu and local Javanese stories. Prambanan was damanged over time by earthquakes but in recent times has been restored.

The Dutch in Indonesia
The Dutch arrived in Indonesia long before pilgrims set sail for America or Captain Cook reached the east coast of Australia. When they arrived in Java in 1596 it was a thriving sophisticated community ruled by Kingdoms that reached back for thousands of years.

TOP: *Sitting Buddha at Borubudur*
ABOVE: *A Dutch map of Jakarta from around 1780*

SAY IT
IN BAHASA INDONESIA...

Kemerdekaan	Independence
Merdeka!	freedom!
sejarah	history
Presiden	President
rempah-rempah	spices

The Dutch found the spices irresistible and sent big ships to bring them back to the Netherlands. The Dutch slowly took over and ruled Indonesia for nearly 350 years.

The Spice Islands

Due to the new trade in spices, Indonesia became known throughout Europe as the Spice Islands. The islands most famous for the trade in spices were near Ambon in the north east of Indonesia. Some of the spices included cloves, cinnamon and nutmeg.

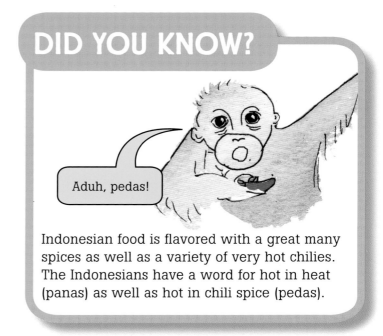

DID YOU KNOW?

Aduh, pedas!

Indonesian food is flavored with a great many spices as well as a variety of very hot chilies. The Indonesians have a word for hot in heat (panas) as well as hot in chili spice (pedas).

DID YOU KNOW?

Indonesian Independence was proclaimed

On the 17th of August 1945 by two prominent leaders of the fight for Independence, Soekarno and Hatta. Indonesian Independence day is celebrated each year.

Indonesian Independence

After the Dutch took control of Indonesia, life changed for many Indonesians. They no longer had freedom in their own country and were often forced to work for

President Soekarno

Dutch masters. Life for some was intolerable. A number of Indonesians started small groups that fought against the Dutch and finally at the end of the Second World War, Indonesia was able to claim independence. Soekarno became the first Indonesian President of Indonesia.

PANCASILA

Indonesia is governed by a set of five basic principles called "Pancasila" and represented by the Garuda bird Coat of Arms.

The five emblems in the middle represent the five principles; The Star (Belief in a God), The Chain (Humanity), The Banyan Tree (Unity), The Bull (Democracy) and The Rice and Cotton (Social Justice). The Garuda bird is a mythical golden eagle found in stories from both Hindu and Buddhist mythology. The Coat of Arms also represents Indonesia's national bird emblem, the endangered Javan-Hawk eagle. The bird's feathers represent the date Independence was claimed.

Look at the Garuda Coat of Arms and try counting the following. What date do you come up with?

1. wing feathers on one side (date)
2. tail feathers (month)
3. the base of the tail (first part of the year)
4. neck feathers (the rest of the year)

New leaders

The second President of Indonesia, Soeharto, took power by force in 1965. He governed the country for 30 years. In 1997 many people reacted against his leadership and he finally stepped down. Since then there have been a few different Presidents.

DID YOU KNOW?

The first-ever female President of Indonesia was Megawati Soekarnoputri, daughter of the first President, Soekarno. She took office in 2000.

Megawati Soekarnoputri, May 2007

Indonesia today has a population of approximately 240 million people. The traditional culture of Indonesia, which has been the same for centuries, exists side by side with new and evolving technologies. Many homes have computers, and Internet Cafes are popular with young people. Young people also love using their mobile/handphone. They can choose to attend a traditional shadow puppet performance or go to the cinema and watch the same movies that you can or enjoy some very good Indonesian movies. There are CD shops that sell CDs from all over the world and shops that sell ipods and computer games. But not everyone can afford the new technology

INDONESIA TODAY

SAY IT
IN BAHASA INDONESIA...

How to count:

1	**satu**	8	**delapan**
2	**dua**	9	**sembilan**
3	**tiga**	10	**sepuluh**
4	**empat**	11	**sebelas**
5	**lima**	12	**dua belas**
6	**enam**	13	**tiga belas**
7	**tujuh**	etc.	

and not all new technologies are available in villages. The contrasts between new and old are every-where.

The Rupiah
The Indonesian money is called *Rupiah.*

Currency rates change all the time. For the most up to date currency rate, check out the Internet where there are currency converters for every country in the world. See how much you could buy today with 10,000 rupiahs!

I'm rich!!

It's only a dollar!

DIFFERENT BELIEFS

Beliefs and religion play a major part in Indonesian life. Many traditional beliefs, passed down from the ancestors have been incorporated into the religions. The main religions include Islam, Hindu, Protestant, Catholic and Buddhist.

DID YOU KNOW?

Before you enter a mosque you must take off your shoes. It is also a requirement in most mosques that you wash your hands and feet at taps provided before kneeling down on small mats to pray.

Islam

Islam first came to Indonesia via traders from as early as the 7th century but did not become widespread until the 14th century onwards. Now the majority of people in Indonesia follow the Islamic religion.

The place of worship for Islamic followers is called a mosque. Muslims are expected to pray five times a day. The call of the mosque, a haunting melody sung by a male singer, awakens you from a deep sleep at approximately 4:00 AM for the first prayer time every morning. In the morning the family prays in their own home—kneeling down and facing Mecca, where Islam is said to have originated. During the day children can pray at school and people can pray in special rooms at their workplace. Friday is a special day and many businesses, shops and schools close early so that people can visit the mosque to pray and attend other ceremonies or celebrations.

LEFT: *The Islamic holy book is called the Koran (Qu'ran).*

RIGHT: *Islamic bride in Java wearing a headdress made entirely of perfumed flowers. Can you imagine how beautiful the aroma would be?*

Jilbab

Many Islamic women and girls choose to wear a head covering when they leave their home. In Indonesia this is called a jilbab and can be white or different colors. Not all Islamic women in Indonesia wear the jilbab and some choose to wear a different form of covering.

Islamic greeting

In Indonesia when you greet someone from the Islamic community you give the greeting "assalamu'alaikum" which means "Peace be with you."

They reply "walaikum salam" which means the greeting is received and returned in peace.

Ramadan

Ramadan is the traditional fasting month for Islamic people all over the world. Except for young children, the elderly and sick, every-one fasts from sunrise to sunset each day.

During the fasting month, visiting relatives is expected. Many people who work in the city return home to their village to visit family. Steamed rice cooked in woven ba-nana leaves (ketupat) or a special chicken dish made with coconut milk (opor ayam) are presented as gifts to your relatives when you visit them. After the last fasting day great celebrations are held and special feasts are prepared.

Ketupat

Making the ketupat woven basket is not easy. Look at the photos on this page and see how the ketupat maker weaves the coconut leaves into a little basket that can contain the rice.

Budhist temple in Java.

Buddhism

Many people, especially those who originate from China, follow the Buddhist religion. Buddhist pilgrims also came to Indonesia in the 8th Century and built the ancient Bud-dhist temple, Borobudur. (see page 25) A special Buddhist celebration and gathering is held each year at the Borobudur monument.

Protestant and Catholic

The Portuguese traders and later the Dutch brought the Christian religion to various parts of Indonesia. Flores in east Java for example is mostly Catholic whereas some parts of Sumatra are Protestant.

Hindu-Bali

The Hindu religion was first introduced into Indonesia by traders that came from India between the 8th and 10th centuries. Apart from small influences elsewhere, the only place in Indonesia where those beliefs remain is Bali.

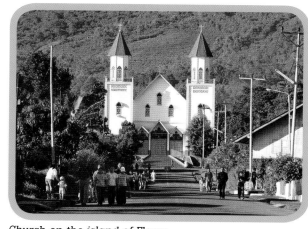

Church on the island of Flores

Many local Balinese beliefs and traditions were adapted into the Hindu religion, making a unique set of beliefs tied in closely with music, dance, art and ritual. It is often referred to as the Hindu-Bali religion and is followed by the majority of people on the island.

The Balinese believe in many gods and spirits that live in the mountains, the rice fields and sea. Apart from large ceremonies that are conducted a number of times throughout the year, each Balinese family also make their own offerings to their gods and goddesses every day. In the rice fields offerings are made to the rice goddess, Dewi Sri, so that a good harvest is ensured. Offerings are also placed on footpaths, outside shops or home to ensure that the good spirits remain.

Birth and death in Bali

While celebrating the rites of passage—from birth through death—are part of many traditions in Indonesia, the celebrations that take place in Bali are some of the most elaborate. The first of these ceremonies happens even before a baby is born, when a mother is 5 months pregnant. People in Bali experience many rites and celebrations throughout their lives. Death is celebrated with the cremation ceremony—the burning of the body so that the soul or spirit may be released to return as another life form.

SAY IT
IN BAHASA INDONESIA...

mesjid	mosque
gereja	church
pura	Balinese temple
agama	religion
adat-istiadat	customs and beliefs

Offerings often consist of a small portion of rice, a piece of fruit, a colorful flower and burning incense.

LEFT: *Decorations for the Kuningan celebration*
RIGHT: *Offerings are brought to the temple on Kuningan.*

Hari Galungan

Galungan in Bali is a special celebration and lasts for 10 days and occurs every 210 days according to the Balinese calendar. It is at this time that it is believed the Balinese gods descend from above and visit earth. They leave again on the last day of celebrations, called Kuningan. It is also believed that the spirits of the family's ancestors return to their former homes. Suitable prayers and offerings are prepared for their visit. Throughout the final day of celebrations temples on the island are

In Bali, the garden, the courtyard and the shrine are all part of the temple. The multi-tiered thatched roof of the shrine is typical in Bali.

crowded with people bringing elaborate offerings which they have been preparing in the days beforehand. The day after is a time for families to enjoy time together or go out somewhere together.

Selamatan

A Selamatan is a ceremony held through-out the islands of Indonesia but is particu-

Indonesian proverb
Bagai telur diujung tanduk! (like an egg on the end of a horn!). Meaning that there is a critical situation— one move and the egg will be punctured.

Cicak bagai telur diujung tanduk!

larly popular in Java. This ceremony celebrates and offers good luck for such things as the birth of a child, the building of a new house, the opening of a new building or for musicians before a performance. Family, neighbors and friends all gather to cel-ebrate together. Special food is prepared including yellow rice in the shape of a cone

(nasi tumpeng). Everyone sits on bamboo mats on the floor around where the food has been placed. Offerings with the sweet aroma of burning incense are placed nearby. The person organizing the ceremony provides a speech and sometimes says a prayer. Afterwards the guests chat together while eating a portion of nasi tumpeng provided on individual plates for each guest.

Sumatra

LEFT: *Traditional costume for the Minangkabau region of Sumatra. This costume is worn in different variations for weddings or other traditional ceremonies.*

RIGHT: *Traditional costume from the Batak region of Sumatra. This is a traditional wedding costume with both couples wearing the long wide scarf called 'ulos' and a woven cloth called mandar which is worn like a sarong. The ulos may be worn in different ways and sometimes just over one shoulder of the bride. Sometimes the man wears a white shirt under his costume.*

TRADITIONAL
REGIONAL COSTUMES

In Indonesia there many colorful and elaborate traditional costumes from different regions and islands. At one time these costumes were worn every day. Now, most young people dress in western style for everyday, but still wear their colorful traditional costumes for special occasions. Many of the costumes include specially dyed fabrics or hand-woven and embroidered materials. Sometimes they include special types of headdress or hair ornaments.

Java

Traditional costume for men and women in Java. There are many regional variations of this costume. The top worn by the women is called 'kebaya' and varies in length and style throughout Indonesia.

Bali

LEFT: *This costume is typical of the clothing worn by men and women on their wedding day in Bali.*

ABOVE: *This lady is wearing the type of costume worn at traditional temple ceremonies in Bali.*

RIGHT: *These Balinese girls are carrying offerings of fruit upon their heads as they walk to the temple dressed in national costume.*

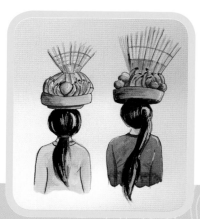

DID YOU KNOW?

If you want clothes you can also easily drop into a "Tailor's"– usually a small store where clothes are made and if you don't have a pattern, a page with the latest fashion from a magazine will do.

Sulawesi

In Sulawesi, this costume is typical of that worn by men and women at traditional ceremonies, including weddings and funerals.

GETTING AROUND

Types of transport

Finding transport to take you to various places is easy in Indonesia. There are all kinds of vehicles to choose from. If someone wants to go to the market in the morning and will need help bringing the produce back home, they can wave for a *becak*. As the *becak* has no gears, the driver takes the flattest route possible and takes only one or two passengers. Passengers who don't know the price of the ride must ask, and will often bargain the price down.

Not all transport requires bargaining. Only small vehicles such as the *becak* and horse and cart require the bargaining to take place before you get on

board. Other transport has a set price—and the money is paid to a person who collects the money for the driver. On the small vehicles called *bemos* or colts (like mini vans) the money collector is also the person who hangs out the door as the vehicle drives along its route and tries to find passengers. Often the *bemo* might look full but the money collector knows just how to push one more person in.

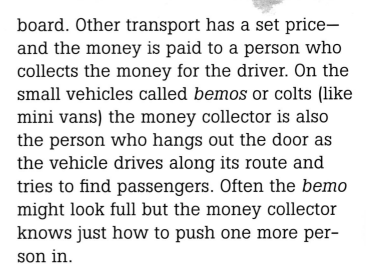

Passenger: To the market, please. And could you wait for me outside the market. How much is the fare?
Becak driver: 6,000 Rupiahs.
Passenger: Oh – that is way too high. How about 2,000 rupiahs?
Becak driver: (Shaking his head) 4,000 rupiahs.
Passenger: 3,000
Becak driver: 3,500.
Passenger: Ok

There are also bus stops where you can wait for the bigger city buses.

Trains travel all over Java but are not found all over Indonesia.

To travel from Jakarta to Bali you can take a train then a bus and then a ferry. The bus trip is usually one that no one forgets. While the scenery is beautiful, it's the speed of the ride that is likely to have you hanging onto the edge of your seat.

You might not be surprised, therefore, when you see a bus being blessed before its journey in Bali. A small offering to the gods is often placed on the bus before departure.

The *dokar* is a two wheeled horse and cart. The *andong* is a larger four-wheeled horse and cart found mostly in the area of Yogyakarta in Central Java.

The horse and carts are very skilled at getting around motorbikes, cars and buses in towns but can also be found in the quieter streets of hillside villages where driving a *becak* would be impossible. It is a very peaceful way of traveling.

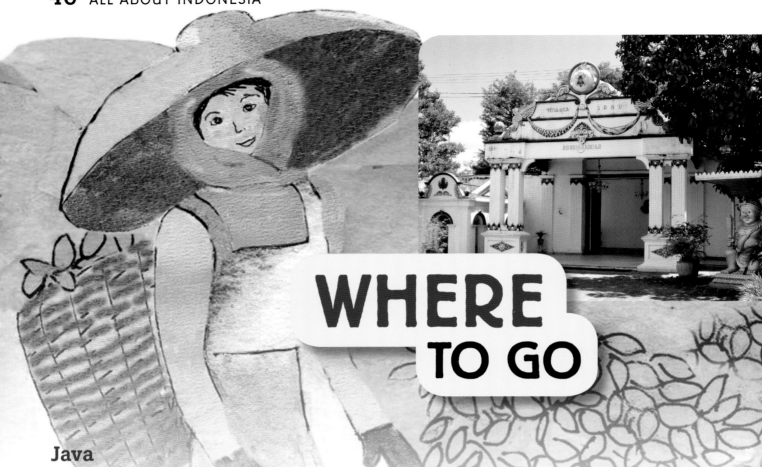

WHERE TO GO

Java

On weekends families like to escape the heat of Jakarta and head up to Bogor, which is a few degrees cooler. On the way they pass through the famous tea gardens. Tea is grown across large areas high up on the mountain slopes near Bogor. At a place called Puncak Pass—you can stop for a rest, have a cup of tea and a snack, breath in the cool mountain air before resuming your journey.

Bogor is also famous for its wonderful Botanical Gardens. One of the popular attractions is the Rafflessia flower (Rafflessia arnoldii), shown above, which is the largest flower in the world. It is found in the forests of Sumatra and flowers only once every seven years. It is a very unusual flower that belongs to the carnivorous family of plants (insect eating). Don't get too close to it

DID YOU KNOW?

Tea is a common drink all over Indonesia. In the west of Java they drink their tea without sugar but by the time you reach central Java, the tea is as sweet as syrup. It is served black and hot with a little lid—to keep the heat in and the ants (who have a fondness for sugar) out.

LEFT TO RIGHT: *Sultan's palace, an elaborate gold ceiling inside the palace, and celebrations around the palace*

though! It has a powerful rotting smell that attracts the insects. This one is so large that it can also eat very small animals!

Yogyakarta is often described as the art and music town of Central Java. Here you can find a rich array of traditional cultural entertainment as well as arts and crafts that include delicate silver work, batik art (see page 56) as well as traditional gamelan music.

In Yogyakarta you can also find the Sultan's palace. While he is still called The Sultan, and is greatly respected by the people, he does not hold power like a Sultan used to hundreds of years ago. His palace is traditional in style, consisting of a number of highly decorated buildings in a private courtyard. In one building—shaped with high roof and no walls—there is a very old set of gamelan instruments that are only played once a year at a special festival called Sekaten.

The main street of Yogyakarta, Malioboro street, is lined with shops as well as market stalls selling items mostly for visitors to the town.

Sulawesi

Sulawesi is an unusual shaped island reached by boat or small plane. The people who live in the southern end of Sulawesi are known as the Buginese and are famous for the large wooden boats that they build. These are the same boats that can be seen in the harbor in Jakarta.

In the Tana Toraja region, one aspect of the culture that has become famous is the special elaborate ceremonies held when a person dies. Sometimes funeral celebrations last for a week with many dance performances and a special feast before the cremation takes place.

In the past, life size effigies (representations of those who had died) were sculptured and placed on shelves carved into the cliffs. Smaller bamboo and cloth effigies are created today.

Kalimantan

Kalimantan is the Indonesian name for the island of Borneo. On this island there is an area called Sabah, which is owned by Malaysia, as well as a small area called Brunei, which is ruled by the Sultan of Brunei. As Kalimantan is so large, travel across the island and through the forests can be difficult. The communities that live deep in the forest regions of Kalimantan are known as the "Dayak" people. They rely totally on the river system to transport their produce and to visit other communities.

Effigies on a wall in Tana Toraja, Sulawesi

Traditional houses in Sulawesi

Ambon

Ambon was very famous during the height of the spice trade—when the Portuguese and Dutch used large sailing boats to carry huge barrels of spices back to their homeland. The spices grown in the area included nutmeg, cloves and cinnamon. Ambon was taken over by the Japanese during the Second World War. There is a special memorial cemetery in Ambon to remember the thousands of soldiers who died there in battle against the Japanese.

Bali

Bali is a small island with lush tropical scenery, dominated by Gunung Agung, the island's largest volcano. This volcano last erupted in 1961, killing thousands of people who had

just gathered at the foot of the mountain to celebrate a special Hindu–Bali ceremony held only every 100 years. At the foot of the mountain is the largest Hindu temple on the island. This is called Besakih Temple.

Ubud, a village situated near the cool of the mountains is a popular place for tourists to visit. Here you can visit the "Monkey Forest" and feed the monkeys. Watch out though—they can be very cheeky and jump on your shoulder looking for peanuts.

Flores

Flores is one of many islands east of Bali. On this island there is a famous mountain called Keli Mutu which has three different colored lakes on top. When the sunlight bounces on the water they shine like beautiful green, blue or red jewels. The lakes are part of what is known as a *caldera*. This is a big hole that is left after a volcano blows itself up. The inside collapses and it fills with water and creates a lake. In this case there

Colored lakes from Flores

are three lakes—and the colors are a mystery but thought to be created from the volcanic minerals and sulphur that still rise up into the water.

Lake Toba

Sumatra

Sumatra is one of the larger islands of Indonesia. The culture, traditions, music and language vary across the island.

Lake Toba

Lake Toba in North Sumatra—created from the crater of an enormous ancient volcano, is one of the largest lakes in the world. In the middle of the lake is a small island, called Samosir. The people who live near Lake Toba are

The world's largest caldera lake is found in Indonesia. Lake Toba on the island of Sumatra is 100km long and 30km wide. The lake is one of the deepest in the world and is 450 meters deep in some parts. It was formed between 70,000 and 75,000 years ago after an ancient explosion of a massive volcano.

called the Batak people. Their traditional homes are very distinctive and are built high above the ground.

Minangkabau

In Central Sumatra is the town of Padang. This area is famous for its extremely spicy hot food. The people who live in this area are called 'Minangkabau'.

The traditional Minangkabau house has a high sweeping roof in the shape of a buffalo horn (see the story about the Minangkabau on page 46). Often several families will share one house and as it is built up high, there is room under the house for the farm animals to shelter. A rice barn is also attached to the front of the house.

Aceh

Aceh is situated on the far northern part of Sumatra. The Islamic religion in Indonesia began here hundreds of years ago before its influence spread to other parts of Indonesia. Aceh today still has the strongest Islamic following in Indonesia.

In 2004, the area of Aceh and its capital, Banda Aceh was devastated by a tsunami that killed nearly 130,000 people and left almost 500,000 homeless. The massive 30 meter (100ft) wave was the result of an earthquake that occurred just off the coast of Sumatra.

Minangkabau story

The Minangkabau story is about a victorious buffalo that has come to symbolize the culture, finding its way into the shape of the roofs of the houses and the headdress of the traditional female costume (see page 36).

The word "Minang Kabau" means '"The buffalo wins" or "victorious buffalo." The story goes like this.   Over 600 years ago the King of Java sent a message to West Sumatra announcing his rule of the whole of Indonesia. He ordered them to surrender or they would be killed. The West Sumatrans did not want fight to their death, nor did they want to give up the land of their ancestors. So they gathered together to work out the best way to oppose the king.

After many days of discussion they sent a message to the king that they would sort this out with a buffalo fight. If the king's buffalo won the people of West Sumatra would become his servants; if their buffalo won the king must allow them to live free.

The king, a little surprised at the request but sure of winning with the fiercest buffalo he could find, decided to agree.

The people from West Sumatra had planned their strategy very carefully. They did not choose a large, fierce buffalo. They chose a small calf. They kept it away from its mother for several days and attached daggers to its horns.

The day for the great battle arrived. The two buffalos could not have been more different. In the arena, the king's fierce bull stood strong, ready to fight, stirring up the dust with his hooves. Opposite him stood a little calf. The king laughed. How stupid these people are, he thought—my buffalo will win easily.

However, the little calf was so hungry that it thought this buffalo looked like its mother. In a split second it put its head down and ran straight at the bull, hoping to find its mother's milk. The sharp daggers pierced the belly of the fierce bull and it instantly fell and died. The king was stunned! The West Sumatrans all shouted "Minang kabau" as they danced into the arena and put a wreath around the neck of the victorious calf and led him back to his mother. The West Sumatrans have been known under the name "Minangkabau" ever since.

Modern

In Indonesia there are modern pop and rock bands just like all over the world. Indonesia also hosts the world-known "Idol" and each year chooses their own "Indonesian Idol." There is also a rich culture of traditional music that varies between islands and between regions.

Traditional

Gamelan

Gamelan is a music ensemble consisting of instruments mostly made from bronze. There are gamelan ensembles found in West, Central and East Java, and Bali. They are all different and have a different sound.

Central Javanese Gamelan. Clockwise from top left: Bonang barung , Bonang panerus , Kenong , Rebab , Gambang, Gender, Saron , Slenthem, Kendang

PERFORMING ARTS
MUSIC

Central Javanese gamelan

In Central Java a gamelan ensemble is quite big and usually has between 12 and 25 players and singers. In the pictures on page 47 you can see the types of instruments that make up a gamelan ensemble. The music is often used to accompany traditional dancing or shadow puppet performances (*wayang kulit*). The sound of the music can be described as either soft, like rippling bells, or loud, with metallic rhythmic melodies.

In the pictures on page 47 you can see

Balinese gamelan

DID YOU KNOW?

In Bali there are also bamboo gamelans, which produce a very different sound from bronze gamelans.

The musicians sit on mats on the floor and play their instruments with wooden or cloth bound mallet. The only stringed instrument, the two stringed *rebab*, is played with a bow made of horsehair. Sometimes there is also a bamboo flute called *suling*. Children learn to play gamelan at a young age. There are also special music and art schools and colleges of the arts where traditional music is taught.

Balinese gamelan

Balinese gamelan music is faster and more vibrant than the gamelan music of Java. It is loud so is usually performed outdoors. The instruments play interlocking rhythms that together produce the melody.

Angklung

Angklung instruments are made from bamboo and are shaken to create the sound. They are played in groups and each instrument—a structure that includes two differently-sized tubes—is tuned to a different note. To play a song, each person has to shake their instrument at the right time when their note appears, kind of like a bell choir.

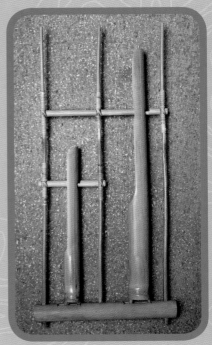

Angklung

One popular dance is called Legong and is danced by three young female dancers.

Bali

Traditional dance in Bali is very colorful and fast. The performers wear elaborately decorated costumes. Their hands and eyes dart back and forth as they move to the rhythmic music. Young children learn to dance from a very young age.

In the Barong dance, the mask and costume has two men underneath who operate the body and dance as the arms and legs. In this story there are humorous characters too, such as the monkey who tries to pick fleas off the restless barong.

The Barong dance

PERFORMING ARTS
TRADITIONAL DANCE

Sumatra

Dancing in Sumatra varies from region to region. One famous dance from the region of Aceh is called the saman dance. The performers kneel in a row on the floor and slowly start a rhythmic routine that involves clapping, slapping their thighs, raising their arms quickly at the same time as singing a song. Sometimes when they turn, their arms interlock with the person next to them, so timing is crucial. The music gets faster and faster until the performers are just a blur.

SAY IT
IN BAHASA INDONESIA...

musik	music
bermain musik	to play music,
tarian	dance
menari	to dance

Central Java

Dance in Central Java is slow and refined and accompanied by gamelan music. The dance usually represents stories taken from the traditional Hindu stories called The Ramayana and Mahabharata (see the section on Shadow puppets on page 52).

Topeng Cirebon

Topeng Cirebon is a dance that is special to the town of Cirebon in West Java. It is mostly danced by men but can also be danced by women. During the performance the dancer wears a special costume and a mask. The dancer transforms through the various personalities of the five panji masks (shown below)—the movements of the dance changing depending on what mask the dancer is wearing. Can you guess the type of personality the red mask might have?

How to make a "Topeng" mask

Topeng means 'mask' in Indonesian. There are Topeng dances from many regions of Indonesia but perhaps two of the most famous are Topeng Cirebon (West Java) and topeng Bali.

You will need:

- a balloon
- strips of newspaper
- paint (different colors including white and black)
- paintbrush (large and fine)
- wallpaper glue made from flour and water
- string
- fine sandpaper

What do do:

1. Blow up the balloon. Tear strips of newspaper and soak in the paste. Cover half the balloon with several layers of newspaper strips. Create a nose from extra strips of newspaper and paste. Let the mask dry.

2. Pop the balloon. Smooth any edges of your mask with the fine sandpaper.

3. Cut a slit for the eyes in the position as shown. Cut another slit for the mouth.

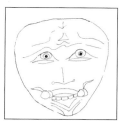

4. Paint the mask with several layers of white paint until no newspaper shows through. Let the paint dry.

5. Draw the details of the mask as shown. Try to make sure the centers of the eyes are painted right above the centers of the slit eye slits. Paint the circular disks near the mouth or attached painted circles of cardboard or large buttons.

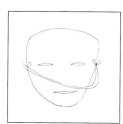

6. Turn your mask over and make two small holes as shown. Get someone to help you measure the string across the back of your head and then tie the end.

7. If you want to look even more like a topeng dancer—thread a series of red pompoms onto a long string and let them hang down each side.

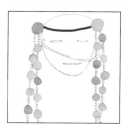

PUPPET SHOWS

Wayang kulit

Shadow puppet performances are popular in Indonesia. The puppets are made from buffalo hide and are carefully crafted so that light can penetrate through the tiny holes. They are also painted beautiful colors.

At a shadow puppet performance, which can take place inside or outside, the audience sits on bamboo mats on the floor in front of a large

white cloth screen. The *dhalang* (puppeteer) sits on the other side with the musicians. The shadow is projected onto the screen via a lamp that hangs on the puppeteer's side.

The clown puppets called Gareng, Semar and Petruk are very funny and often make jokes about the audience or famous people. Children love this part of the performance but find it very hard to stay awake for the whole performance—falling

The story of the forest

A famous story often used in Shadow plays and traditional dance comes from the Ramayana or Mahabharata stories that originated from India. Within each of these long epics there are several shorter tales that can be turned into a shadow puppet performance. One well known story from the Ramayana, tells of Prince Rama and his princess wife, Sita who were banished to the jungle as part of Rama's step mother's cunning plan to have her own son crowned King. In the forest an evil giant, Rahwana, kidnaps Sita. In his long search for his beloved wife, Rama meets and helps Hanoman, King of the monkeys. Hanoman, in return, discovers where Sita is held and sends thousands of monkeys to accompany Rama to fight and overcome Rahwana. The story ends with the freedom of Sita, the prince and princess returning to their home and being greeted with much joy before Rama is pronounced King.

asleep amongst the musicians who keep playing till dawn. A traditional performance can last from 9pm at night till 5am next morning! Sometimes there are shorter ones for visitors.

Wayang golek

These wooden puppets which are shown on the right come from West Java. They are not Shadow puppets but perform some of the same stories.

Wayang kancil

The kancil stories like the one you read on page 17 are sometimes performed with shadow puppets. This is called Wayang kancil.

Pak Ledjer is a famous wayang kancil puppetter in Yogyakarta, Central Java. He has created many different puppets that appear in the different kancil stories.

How to make a kancil and buaya puppet
Try making your own kancil and buaya (crocodile) puppet and turn the kancil story on page 17 into a shadow puppet performance.

You will need:
- cardboard
- glue
- scissors
- paper fasteners
- sate sticks (wooden kebab sticks with the sharp ends cut off)
- thin dowel/cane or bamboo
- masking tape

How to make:
1. Photocopy and enlarge the image of the kancil and buaya.*
2. Glue to the cardboard and trim.
3. Use the paper fasteners to attach the legs to the body of the kancil and buaya as shown. Attach the sate sticks to the legs (and mouth of buaya) with masking tape.

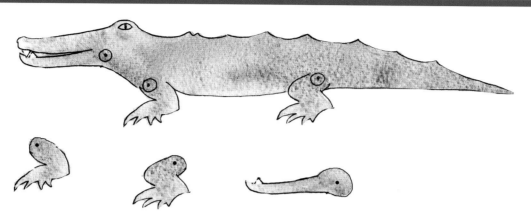

4. Attach the dowel/cane or bamboo to the body of the animal as shown. This is what you hold with your right hand while you manipulate the smaller sticks with your left hand and make the puppet come to life.

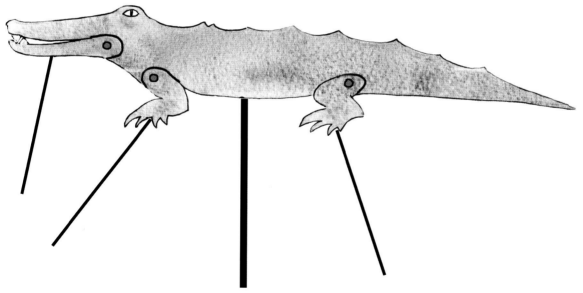

You can make your own shadow puppet theater by cutting away the top and bottom of a cardboard box (be sure to choose a box big enough to fit the scene) and tape a large piece of white fabric or white tissue paper across the bottom to make a screen. Put the box screen side out on a table or other surface and light it from behind

* or visit this book's page on www.tuttlepublishing.com for a printable pdf

Bali is particularly famous for its wooden carvings.

Indonesia has a great variety of arts and crafts. There are beautiful wood carvings, cloth weaving and paintings.

Traditional silverwork

Yogyakarta in Central Java is famous for its intricate silverwork. The craftsmen and women create delicate bracelets as well as beautiful model sailing ships or horse and carriages.

TOP: *Yogyakarta in Central Java is famous for its intricate silverwork. The craftsmen and women create delicate bracelets as well as beautiful model sailing ships or horse and carriages*

ABOVE: *Many islands create beautiful woven cloth. This one comes from Maluku. Woven cloth such as this one are called ikat.*

Batik

Batik is a process of applying wax and colored dyes to cloth. The cloth is dyed and waxed several times until the required color scheme is reached. The wax is then removed (boiled off), leaving a beautiful design. It is most common in Java.

The women usually create traditional style batik while men often create modern batik paintings. Children learn to do batik at school.

How to make batik

The instrument used to draw the wax onto the cloth is called a *canting* (pronounced chan-ting). In Indonesia the wax is heated on a small kerosene stove. Some modern artists use electric frying pans because it can remain at a constant temperature.

For this activity, however, you are not going to use a canting and you are not going to dip the cloth into a dye bath. We are going to use a paintbrush to paint on the wax and a paintbrush to paint on the dye. This is because this method involves cold wax (much safer than hot wax!).

You will need:
- a piece of white cotton cloth (preferably already hemmed around the edges)
- a pencil
- 3 different color cloth dyes (eg. light blue, green, deep purple or black)
- large and small paint brushes (for dye)
- cold wax (available at art stores)
- knife for scraping off wax (with adult supervision)
- newspaper (to keep work space clean)

What do do:

1. Draw your design on your cloth. Try a design that has a combination of thin and wide lines. Paint the parts you want to remain white with coldwax. Allow the wax to dry.

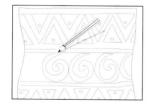 

2. Paint the lightest color dye (light blue) over the whole cloth. Allow to dry.

3. Paint wax over the areas you want to remain light blue. Allow wax to dry.

4. Paint the next darkest color (green) over the whole cloth. Allow to dry.

5. Paint wax over the areas you want to remain green. Allow to dry.

6. Paint the last dye color (deep purple or black) over the last remaining parts of the cloth. Allow to dry.

7. Carefully scrape the wax off. Your batik is complete. Stretch onto frame or just hang in front of a window and watch the sunlight glow through the colors. Some dyes fade in the sun, so be careful not to leave in direct sunlight.

A dish of sate with gado-gado

ENJOYING A MEAL

Indonesian food is flavored with tasty spices and usually has lots of chili. Sometimes chili is an ingredient in the meal, and other times a chili sauce (sambal) is served "on the side." The sauce is very hot, so it's better to try just a little bit at first. Children in Indonesia usually eat milder foods until they are little older.

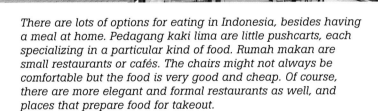

There are lots of options for eating in Indonesia, besides having a meal at home. Pedagang kaki lima are little pushcarts, each specializing in a particular kind of food. Rumah makan are small restaurants or cafés. The chairs might not always be comfortable but the food is very good and cheap. Of course, there are more elegant and formal restaurants as well, and places that prepare food for takeout.

SAY IT
IN BAHASA INDONESIA...

pedas	hot in spice
panas	hot in heat
enak	delicious
Saya suka makan nasi	I like to eat rice

Some well-known dishes are *sate* (marinated meat on skewers cooked over coals and served with a delicious peanut sauce); *nasi goreng* (fried rice); *gado-gado* (steamed vegetables with a peanut sauce and served with slices of cucumber and tomato).

Prawn cracker (*krupuk*) are also served with meals. Fried *tahu* (made from soy beans) is a common accompaniment to some meals. You might know this as the Japanese name, tofu.

DID YOU KNOW?

The hottest food (most spicy) in Indonesia comes from a region called Padang in Sumatra.

CLOCKWISE FROM TOP LEFT: *Some think the taste of a pawpaw is a little like a mango, while others think it tastes more like a banana; Indonesia supplies many of the pineapples enjoyed around the world; Manga (mangoes) are deliciously refreshing and come in several varieties.; Jambu are sweet and are often grown in home gardens.*

FRUITS, DRINKS AND SWEETS

There are many delicious tropical fruits in Indonesia. They include mangoes (manga), pawpaw (papaya), bananas (pisang) and pineapples (nanas) as well as fruits only found in Indonesia.

Rambutan means "hairy" in Indonesian. The skin with the "hairy bits" is peeled off to reveal a white fleshy seed. The taste is sweet and similar to a lychee. Indonesian children love to eat Rambutan just like you might like to eat grapes.

DID YOU KNOW?

The durian smells so bad that some places have signs that say "No Durian allowed!" Indonesians usually love the fruit but visitors find it hard to get past that smell.

Durian has stubby spikes on the outside. Inside the segments of fruit are soft and creamy. The taste is very interesting but the smell can be quite off-putting!

LEFT: *Nangka (jackfruit) are very large. The segments inside have a sweet taste.*

Special drinks and sweets

Fruits such as *nanas* (pineapple) and *jeruk* (lemon) are made into delicious cold drinks. Another particularly refreshing drink is called *es kelapa muda* and is made from young coconuts.

The avocado, which you can buy in most western grocery stores, is a very healthy fruit. Avocado shakes (called Jus Alpukat) are very popular in Indonesia. These delicious drinks usually include some form of chocolate syrup that has been swirled in after the fruit and milk have been blended together. Here's an easy version you can make with or without the chocolate sauce.

Avocado drink

Ingredients:

1 ripe avocado
2 teaspoons white sugar
1 cup of cold milk. You can use regular milk or, if you like your drink a little sweeter, condensed milk can be used. Or try using half a cup of each.
Chocolate syrup to taste (optional)

How to make:

Crush avocado with a fork or use a processor. Add the sugar and cold milk. Mix thoroughly. This is a thick drink but add more milk if the drink is too thick for a straw! Enjoy.

Manisan—Sweet treats

Indonesians don't really have a "sweet" after a main meal. Sometimes fresh fruit is eaten after a meal. But there are sweets that can be eaten at any time of the day and they are delicious! Some are made with sticky rice, others from ground rice flour and most use palm sugar as the sweetener. Some that are popular with children include *pisang goreng* (bananas fried in a batter), *es campur* (a sweet mixture of fruits, coconut milk, palm sugar, condensed milk and crushed ice) and *dadar gulung*.

SAY IT
IN BAHASA INDONESIA...

makan	to eat
minum	to drink
makanan	food
minuman	drink
Saya suka minum jus.	I like to drink juice.
Selamat makan	happy eating

FROM LEFT: *A yummy dish of es campur; This pisang goreng has a sweet crisp batter shell. Inside, the banana is very soft and sweet; Dadar Gulung (green pancake) has a sweet coconut filling. Below is an easy recipe for making your own.*

Dadar gulung

You'll need to use your stove, so be sure to get your parents' permission and supervision when making this sweet treat.

You will need:

Filling:
- 2 cups fresh grated coconut (or dessicated coconut from a packet)
- 10 tablespoons grated palm sugar (or dark brown sugar)
- 1 cinnamon stick, break in half
- ¼ teaspoon salt

Pancake:
- 1½ cup rice flour (or plain flour)
- 1¾ cups coconut milk
- ½ teaspoon salt
- 1 egg beaten
- 3 drops of green food coloring (originally this was colored with pandan leaf paste)
- vegetable oil or butter for frying

What do do:

Mix the grated coconut, sugar, cinnamon and ½ teaspoon salt together. Fry the mixture in a small pan over medium/low heat, constantly stirring for approx 5 minutes or until mixture is dry. Remove the cinnamon stick and set it aside.

Mix the flour, coconut milk, ½ teaspoon salt, green food coloring and egg into a smooth batter. Lightly oil a fry pan and pour approximately 3 tablespoons of the batter into the pan. Make sure the pan is equally covered with the batter so that the pancake is thin and even. Fry for one minute, turn the pancake over and fry for another minute until cooked. Remove and set aside.

To fill the pancake. Place 2 tablespoon of the filling near the edge of the pancake. Fold over once, then tuck in the left and the right sides and fold over once more. Press gently to ensure the filling is evenly spread. Serve. Makes 10–12 servings.

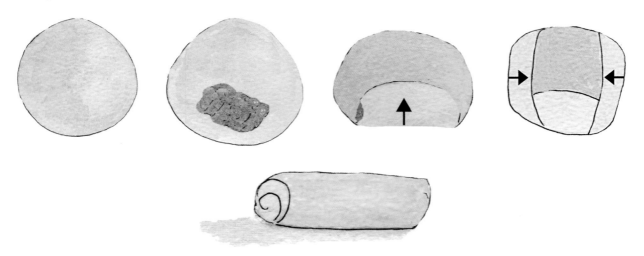

Sampai jumpa lagi
Until we meet again

Ge -------lang si pa ku ge ----- lang ge---------

lang si ra --------- --- ma ra---------ma Pu---

lang ma ri lah pu lang Ma --- ri----lah pu

lang ber--- sa----- ma----sa------ma. Pu-lang pu

lang ma--- ri---- lah pu-----lang Ma----ri - lah pu----

lang ber ----sa---ma-----sa-------------- ma.

SAY IT
IN BAHASA INDONESIA...

Selamat jalan goodbye to the person leaving

Selamat tinggal goodbye to the person staying

Sampai jumpa lagi until we meet again

pulang to return home

There are many different translations of this song. Whilst originating as a harvesting song and sometimes accompanying a candle dance, it is also a popular "farewell" song. If you wanted to sing some English words, try the following.

The harvest rice has been stored. We join to celebrate the day.
Too soon it's harvest, time to go home
Come let us go home, together we'll go.
Alas, too soon, it's time to go home.
Come, let us go home. Together we'll go.

Acknowledgments

I especially want to thank the main photographer for this project, my long time friend, Asita Majdi. Her wonderful photographic skills and love of her own culture can be seen in the beautiful photos she took specifically for this book. Her enthusiasm to embrace the project from her home in Yogyakarta and her willingness to help out for all requests was much appreciated.

I would also like to thank Michael Ewing for his inspiration for the Topeng Cirebon section and for providing several photos. Thank you also to; Wendy Miller for her beautiful photos; Emil and Liliana Schmid who kindly allowed their photos to be reproduced; Irene Ritchie for photos included in Wayang Kancil section and Kalimantan; Brynna and Rowan for providing the photograph of the Koran; Julienne Welsh, Barb Slee, Tracey Ferguson and Kris Williamson for their photos.

Thank you also to my first editor, Sandra and to Terri who enthusiastically led the book through to its final stages.

I thank my parents, Marge and Ray, for first introducing me to Indonesia as a child. To my son, Aden, and children everywhere, may this book allow you to catch a glimpse into a country that is rich with diversity.

Index

Photo Credits

Asita Majdi 4, 5, 6 (3rd, 4th, 5th, 6th, 7th and 9th)), 8 (market), 10 (rice growing), 12, 13 (bottom 3), 14, 15, 16, 18 (girl), 19 (all), 22 (all), 23 (middle and bottom), 24 (bottom), 25, 31 (girl and wedding), 32, 38, 39 (all), 40, 41, 58 (all), 59 (bottom two), 61

Emil and Liliana Schmid 4 (top), 13(top), 33, 43 (did you know?)

Julienne Welsh 6 (1st and 8th)

Wendy Miller 49, 50, 52

Kris Williamson 3, 44 (Lake Toba), 45 (Minangkabau houses)

Michael Ewing 7 (Jakarta), 8 (Monas), 9 (top two), 13 (2nd and 3rd from top), 18-19 (school kids top photo), 27, 30, 34, 43 (top and bottom), 50 (topeng), 60

Linda Hibbs 29 (top), 47, 56 (all)

Denise Hibbs 9 (bottom village)

Tracey Ferguson 16,21, 23 (top), 29 (bottom)

Irene Ritchie 16 (orangutan), 42 (both), 53, 54

Rowan Gould and Brynna Rafferty-Brown 31

Jordy Theiller 11 (top)[1]

Thomas Schiet 14 (top)

Gunawan Kartapranata 04 (top)[1]

Bennylin 26 (top)[1]

Yan Arief Purwanto 28 (Magawani Sukarnoputri)[2]

Marcello Casal Jr/ABr 28 (Susilo BambangYudhotono) This photograph was produced by Agência Brasil, a public Brazilian news agency[1]

Spencer Weart 34 (top right)[1]

Scott Bauer 59 (top left, pawpaw) USDA ARS Image K7575-8

Forest & Kim Starr 59 (top right, pineapple) reprinted under Creative Commons Attribution-Share Alike 2.5 Generic license

W.A. Djatmiko 59 (top, lower right, manga)[1]

Brücke-Osteuropa 59 (bottom right, durian) reprinted under Creative Commons CC0 1.0 Universal Public Domain Dedication

mita1409 61 (left)[2]

Midori 61 (center)[1]

1. Reprinted under Creative Commons Attribution-Share Alike 3.0 Unported license
2. Reprinted under Creative Commons Attribution-Share Alike 2.0 Generic license